excisions

excisions

hilary plum

www.blacklawrence.com

Executive Editor: Diane Goettel
Book Design: Amy Freels
Cover Design: Zoe Norvell
Cover Art: "The Unicorn Surrenders to a Maiden (from the Unicorn Tapestries)," Metropolitan Museum of Art, Gift of John D. Rockefeller Jr., 1938

Published 2023 by Black Lawrence Press.
Printed in the United States.

for Caryl

Ghosts don't need to arrange their meetings,
but for you it's still necessary

—Ryoko Sekiguchi, trans. Lindsay Turner

Contents

Cultivated

A garden ends somewhere.
A red bird calls by the mouth
of the cave but the novel ends.
This will be butterflies, this
a flag. Ascend a terrace and limbs
of trees have been trained in an arc
through which air simulates the
oral history of a militia. The letters
of the lovers are always discovered.
Lovers earn the name by awaiting
a letter and the novel only marks
an interval, a cooling key.
At the breakwater lovers
cultivate the cats who slide
out from the rocks to leave
footprints in lake. A handful
of meat on a rock won't feed
you through winter. Winter is
neither symbol nor translation
of key into rust into rose, now
civil war. Like a letter she is
always rediscovered. Watch her
flee through the statuary, outpacing cats
in the eyes of the law of the novel,
where a trench should appear.
A garden commences where you pull
a key from earth, red worm ripening
your skin. Birds descend like red
bullets. Somewhere I found a statue
named for the river you're named for,

a name your ancestors, you told me,
forgot as soon as they uprooted
themselves from its banks.
I have caused you some pain.
Your next letter arrives.

Ambulances

In the reproduction the colors of the cloud
diffused until it stood in for the flesh whose
genes are lately of real interest to professionals.
I used to keep a shirt of yours unwashed
but then you survived. Before a question
of proportion, a nucleus of who draws
the line. The line represents who you are
before the line, a restitution proceeding
as the breakwater delineates wave.
Now our bill is settled by ransom. Your
rights accrete then erode. Once you've
built a prison the cells are more or less
free. The turret encircled us with an ease
we didn't know belonged to another time.
Picture us then. The breakwater a patois
sunset dyes till you forget who paid
for the breakwater. Now you don't
picture anything. I sit at the bedsides
of real dying writers and learn that
I'm scared to die. There is no charge.
I would have called this rupture a lighthouse
but this is what it looks like.

Recall

Was anyone gone
Sirens cross the window
and morning glories bloom

If a nest an ambulance
keeps pace with breaking shells

Like something I knew
the translucence of
the unmoving vein

You were traveling through
a meadow damp with concrete
or a whistle from this ship
down the river

Can't recall the pattern
A pillow some spit
and this foreign dream folded
barely the skin of your cheek at dawn
At the museum you knew
what you would see there

Were we walking
The street shared its name
with a street elsewhere
we'd meant to reach
the end of
If the city divided
each side

would keep streets
A boy running
Fresh dust

By the hour we passed
the edifice, its stones scarred
(the fire had altered the course,
we knew, of history)
each stone was dark

In pane or iris sight pulsed

Agent

Dusted toy soldiers
in the crèche   located silver
spheres of mercury
in glass   scattered glass

Read the heatmap to find
everyone at the covert
base   everyone
in the world with a product
lit up

If you can't say where
dark place like this
that's where   missiles
cereal boxes and missiles
counted pillows

Chose not to tell you about it
no shirt in the kitchen
chose to free the little mouth
from my warm hair

Quick flesh

She moves from farm to town bringing
only daughters. The call of dough thrown
to hot stone. In the butcher's shop she loses
only two fingers, while the vacant
farmhouse on whose porch I was never
pictured vanished. There's little the rich
won't harvest. Wind threshes only an orchard,
in the womb a child burgeons. In the hospital
mother holds the hand of father's body,
which takes two weeks to release the dose
of radiation it may release while alive.
Daughters bear daughters, a dark roof to
the orchard's mouth. There's a sound caught
like a soft piece of lung or a phrase in the old
language for a hand hot on the back,
the back to another cold wall. Across state
lines you followed, quick stitching of an
organ to itself. In town she lost only
one religion. Other daughters watch,
sewing butter to butter. This is the bread
of the body not left for coyotes
and it was birds I first
no longer heard.

Still wife

A triangle began

Car full of voters   mountain nearly removed

In the foreground was I crying

Blue-green the algae   emerging from each pierced

kernel of corn

Crying was still a position

into external spaces like the start

of a kettle's screaming   I'd long seen the mountain

there, where it was   thing in window steam clouded

like salt seals the lid or salt   bricks years up beneath

the mountain

Car steady on the tracks   surface clogs the filter

meant I was there   where you could see me

Car along the orthogonal

You could find me or assume my position

not sounding the opaque shape of pond

not signaling to a V of birds   streaming through

an absence

someone was plummeting

Excisions

In the past, living then in a valley, we climbed. *May we go on a walk?*
But he stays in bed.

Each street had its own architect, so that passing from one block to
another—here rows of glass porches; there again and again veins of
bright mortar—is exiting another's dream.

Emigration, immigration—to change vowels to change point of
view.

I think he has forgotten I am watching the video, he walks along a
corridor and stands, to take a piss, no, he makes an espresso, behind
him rows of containers I cannot read.

The video is not about the past. If you open the door, children will
tumble out, I see them every day in the street.

The doorway bears, in time it collapses. In time you must remove the
child from the womb.

From the vantage point, a cold plane of rock, we saw the fog that
obscured the valley and had no sense of our home, a building with a
balcony near enough to the neighbor's you could light his cigarette,
in each kitchen behind you each spouse.

We left the valley: there is no battle not advantaged by hill.

If each rock on the path was not held in the long belly of a glacier. If you stop feeding it poison the tumor feeds on skin. Skin shines, blood will be red.

I do not think it is immoral, he says, over the hiss of espresso, *I think it is immoral not to speak of it.*

Of the armies who passed through the valley there are a series of plaques. Surgery is one way to distinguish between the incorporeal and the incorporated.

I wouldn't call the valley a wound, though this is where plates would have made a new ocean. When you die your skin will be stitched into no one.

No surprise, your hand, in the night north of the hip. How sharp the hip above the softening belly. If you see the photograph, you see the past.

In the novel this year repeats the same sentence as the year before. I can sleep if he is crying.

I climbed the stairs. In the woods the rustle was two young bucks, hooves quick in the leaves, antlers locked. Only one turned and ran.

Wind tidies the walnuts, forces you to close your eyes. I wouldn't say who has appeared in my dreams, faces he hopes to see.

The flowers stink at different rates, but I throw them out all at once.

Wind casts leaves over the kitchen floor and a wine bottle is still. *One departure came between us and with death*, a line I read in a novel. Through summer I recalled it and not until fall did I know I'd read it wrong.

In a city there are no hospitals, not a failure of planning, a success of bombing. The bathtub would be one place, but he speaks of the woods.

Squirrels nest in the walls. There is a vibrating phone. The woods are mine.

In a novel there is always another life, especially if no one lives it.

The wind is too cold, nipples firm against fabric. To the hospital we take the train, here and there the city delivers us, asking only a spare dollar, another day, a place for two rivers to meet.

This is the point on the map where you start the memoir of your homecoming. Again in the waiting room a woman asks what ppm of tap water may safely be human blood.

I commit to memory a poem I wrote years ago, when the effects of quinine had just dissipated. The woman is redrawing her eye makeup in the exact shades of your own.

Across the floor drops of something pink, a fluid the gut has been secretly making.

In the dream the lover is so young I am embarrassed for him. Later a scholar will exchange *lover* for *mistress* in every appearance.

Later they will close the cafés. You will forget the city—the thigh of the counter girl you watched through the timely rips in her jeans—until it is bombed.

This could mean anything, like the words *historical* or *virus*.

In this case, if you are not with him, he is alone. Nurses write another name on the board.

In their downtime the nurses make pies faster and faster. This connects a night you fucked, wearing only a jean skirt that would later be stolen, to an email on which you were cc'ed today.

From the café wall I, still sentimental, tear a strip from each flyer that bears my name. One result of hours spent in the crucifix position is this swollen hand.

In the room there are people you do not touch. This is what you would never say of the café.

Every letter addressed to *wife* you receive.

For the goose, you advise a bat, for the mouse a trowel or a hand. These incisions in the muscle they call a release.

I was wearing a dress you could spill any drink on, and in this fashion years passed. Our feet were damp.

I recalled the years I sat by the window and watched each neighbor, phone to ear, step back in hope of reception and into the path of a stranger's car. In that region, I told him as he counted day lilies, we killed 400,000 deer per annum just to break even.

If you looked for a jawbone, you found a jawbone. In the water a scar is harder to abrade.

Together we ascended the hill apples rolled down; when I described the crest you watched my face. Some years it still rained.

From there you could hear each coyote in town, you could hear each neighbor call a neighbor, *won't you shut up your dogs.* The doctor's memory is photographic.

She shrouds the tumor with her own hand. The nipple still answers to your description.

Each time we swam the neighbors must have heard, yet we didn't speak of the wash of porch light over our throats.

Really she wasn't a scientist. These days she's a doctor and prays each time she steps foot on shore.

A mile beyond the tomb, a replica of the tomb. A small team, not employed by the king, perfects the smell.

Bacteria redraw each face in the king's retinue as the face of a worker, poised, camera in hand.

A hand lifts hissing coffee through its own steam. The flame is still on. In the video the hand is my own, shaking.

They have found it soothing to arrange along the hospital corridor cardboard cutouts of doctors, nurses, and singing orderlies. The stubble on the face of each resident is accurate at midnight.

It helps to reapply lipstick just as the needle slides home. In all this time I have been working on this sitcom about a family of museum docents who communicate by clasping and unclasping their hands.

The archaeologists were sponsored by competing shoe companies. In the video my hand keeps aging. Each feature of each patient is blurred: you see only the cloth roses that bloom tirelessly from the torso.

Let's say my shadow obscures your face, we call this low budget. Let's say the video is a pretense, foam cupped in the prison barber's palm. The lipstick tastes like the rivulet that reaches the lips from the dome of the scalp.

I offer the lipstick to you, though you had asked only for perfume. Around us in the café people use their hands or their mouths. You would not call them patients, exactly.

In the video you could see this only in infrared. Later they'll build a replica of the café but without the ball bearings.

When the mirror catches the scent of the body, I will no longer face the mirror.

Agent

Woke late
moths changed course when I turned
off   in the night
don't know   what did we
represent

Developer correcting town square's
angles   again
you woke from
recorded sound of train

In time silent to talkies to
cell phone in jail   kids
shouldn't be heard   before
rock   glacier annuls

Chose not to add anything to this
chose to keep it like this

Little autophagy

In the panorama we witnessed little,
though the details were fine. A fractured ulna.
Do you ever just watch the bricks?
the man asked when we found him
in the same position. Only from this angle
did the tumor block light. The skin
of the soldiers looked fresh in the low oil sun.
An effect, we discovered, of gas the painter's
models inhaled. The room was cold,
rings fell from fingers. The man closed his eyes.
I remember, he said, referring to an era
in which men came home from the war
and nobody stood for it. Wherever you stood,
the panorama led you, a townsperson, through
the field, once your field, one day after
the battle, in advance of the photographers
whose portraits of the dead the panorama
recalled. Your hands looked bare.
A fire escape finely heated. For the dead
the man murmured some names.
And this, you said, is no birthday.
These were tents and this was afternoon.
How modern they were, like light off bricks
that very morning. After some time
the field stops moving.
There was, I thought, a narrator.
A hand fresh on an arm. Move along.

Good news

In both cases, the body.
A hysterical ecstasy. A
procedure to remove
the portion of tapestry
in which the unicorn
defends himself.
A maiden watches,
splashed. A pillow,
unwashed. In the
event you squinted, I
translated only texts
in which I appear
in your language my
name in the mark of
you whose face reflects
my appearance. Hounds
bayed. I requested
the same. Sidewalk
stained the city. This is
not what brought us
closer. A wind scented
with stomach acid heads
out to sea. It's routine,
a volume of blood
you could maintain.
Flesh represents
flesh. A single hair
or another. I smelled
of the sea after you
delineated how you

enter the sea. The corniche
hushed, its last sound
this exquisite
gestation.

Lions

The long fact of the turned face is named faith.

Through tall windows opposing the tapestries

that depict the gaze of the lion, low hills with dark cows

remain far. A pheasant plump in the dirt, a voice saying *you*

and modern angles guide us into a room where we were

never again, as in the absence of any machine a man

bends. I hear his regular breath.

You once sent me (just now) a manifesto composed

decades ago, its sloganeering an instrument anyone

tried when damning the candles of the high chandelier.

Never before was I anyone, and still I am revealed

in the glass face of the hallway bookcases I believed

were meant for your use. Beneath the weight of

our error the stone of the dumbwaiter cleaved. At

times the voice of my father assumed a tone of pride.

My hands are declarative between cow and calf

when I seize daily this milk for my own. Leaning long

over the fence, a shadow, a husband whistling lightly,

or a stand of bamboo wind sings through. I tend to turn

toward what I cannot distinguish, cream pursuing the curve

of my calf or the path toward my nipple of your tongue.

The sun sounds like foreign birds.

And someone cut a way through the woods then

watched who took it. Here was chamber, arena, and jail.

Across the field gaze invaded, a page swelling with what

we could at last read. Lungs hissed with dust. Wax hit

hot the floor like a hymn on the still-droning deck.

Today a sky shot through with official witnesses,

whosoever traces the sunlit motions of our texts

against every cell in the firmament,

your eyes in the cobalt-alloyed air.

And I, who have never seen a corpse

You keep

the name siege   orchards of

systems theorized sweetness

they must   and weren't

you   keeper of one

palmful of glistening near sanguine

seeds representing seeds of

pomegranate   one pomegranate

in hand but   released   kept an old image

like a face   a map   animated

a bird through this ripe wind or

something like their whole heaped world

cauterized fruit as it   as if

something to be said for   describing

I   did   release

a tendril   ground held

sap   as memory

Sanctuary on ice

Here the sky angled for monuments
and you passed invisibly through
the intaglio workshop, close noises
of the nearsighted, or snow heaping
up on the flesh of a grapefruit,
imported. While falling I reached
for any wall. Felt your hand or ankle,
some argument I forgot you could make.
I'd tried the drug myself, persistent vacay
in the old colony, each boulder
signifying: here settlers stepped
onto shore, here settlers trained
cannons seaward toward settlers.
You seized my elbow, no one's
choice to implant. Dream of an
appendix, you said, those dreams
never end. Here a mother hurled
dough at each girl until at last,
bread. And the sea composed itself
of each drug we flushed. When you
bent low you saw that every cameo
portrayed the kids' metadata, unique
as an engine made of ice. I was
holding hard onto any NFT, a stick
of sealing wax, melted. I don't go there
anymore, you said, but you meant
we could extract anything through
the keyhole. Now this was offscreen.

If a gun disappears it reappears

Had the sort of job you
couldn't see clearly it was
just money   like
heaving stones no archaeologist
schooled in empire
declines   out of matches
I am building a facsimile
of the city   in the version
of you represented on film
you speak the language
of the disease they invented
the machine to see
            watch
this match gets lit

Canal

Back and forth by the water
strollers grow pinker until
they're shopping carts
              in a museum
the war did not glass
itself up   the name
of your country was changed
glass worn by the force of the tongue
                         you want
the sculpture to be in uniform so
lay your uniform against
the naked lacquer   turn
your name in   turn the corner
to where the air has been
desertified to nourish the sphinx a boat
brought here, an absent boat
wood often softens
          spitglass or bloodglass
figures like yours contest
a gone landscape   airport paved
over uncatalogued birds   or a camp
popularizing that no procurator
enters   song has

a habitat but this is
not song   just resemblance
as each year on what I call
your birthday   you swallow
perfumed ashes   keep
the worms at bay

Startled newspaper

In the living room glossing
backdrop of marriage   motion like
the boarding of a shrimp boat by
some appropriate authorities
          or skin accommodating
a flooding vein   I was running
my hand down a sort of
history, pulp of family names
from which yours had been
excised   above the fold   sunset
over the sole boat to breech
the embargo   forewarned
                    a fate of
vaccinations, basketballs, a long-
awaited incubator   this
name   falling
helicopters, taxis and hypotaxis
sort of bread   plumping in
the inflamed air   between lightning
and thunder   children still
count in a foreign tongue you said
or the report dilated by water
you didn't mention
you didn't own
the whole fleet

Accurate sculpture

I didn't mean to exhibit
the painting   nor use
the same schema to declare a
midpoint in crucifixion,
midpoint in resurrection
                though I took
an interest   swabs and all that
or a sudden vacancy in
menstruation

There are many videos
like the end of a mid-sized city
or the episode in *Escaping Polygamy*
in which only one wife remains

The painting accepts
one protestor   who appears in
each instance you called me to tell
NSA about   and I
negotiated what we had not been
reacting to   mark
on the ribcage, smear on the thigh
          hit replay

From our hill

A flare rising   below
in the passages this is light   like
light anyone could open a door
you were
not there   having never
learned the difference between
camp and city   the difference
is there   another hand
                I read
the newspaper was obscured
after a scrim the hue of flesh never
yours but preferred   as if night
were a room in which your long dream
of my flesh was housed   blinds
low   night lasts   not
a history   but a time you still
recognize, jasmine or rosemary, a peeling
back   a quarry children
still swim in

Excisions

This neighborhood is still known by clouds. You break the silence between us to tell me what becoming immune to my speech has made you immune to.

I finger my own wounds, as not even Christ did. Into the sky bare trees on a ridge are a row of fine lesions. In any hospital if you sit long enough bedside the doctor will call you *mother*.

The irony is that no creature evolved to live in the Arctic may see the colors today's melting allows. Have you had a child, the nurse asks, looking over my shoulder as the video replays on the phone. The irony is that none of them want to go to America. A drone was invented to stay aloft in only this weight of cloud.

I finger the tomb, which artists are only beginning to depict in the new style. The interval is sweet after which I realize the finger in my mouth is the cause of your silence. The irony is that a swipe of the tongue could play the video. When they say encrypted they do not mean the tomb. You would be the one to tell me what the irony is. Artists come to this city for the natural appearance of its technology.

A vacuum necessitates the drain and, in time, the orgasm. The irony is that nothing smells more like you than the fear this architectural moment arose to deny.

Your cries in the night have begun to sound like the Zamboni calming the ice. My apology has the smack of fresh plum against concrete. This sidewalk leads more or less to the lake, where ships haul up sunk ships.

Sometimes I feel the crew has laughed at the wrong time. Sometimes, for no more than our pleasure, the doctor has made a pie.

Could it matter that the only skater is the driver of the Zamboni? We have divided our time into before and after before. I hope to keep moving away, you say, denoting the nonessential. It is only winter that ripples the skin of the fruit.

It is only lobbyists, their teeth smooth as a rink, who call the lake too big to fail. This is before, this is after. This is the work of the Russians. This is the discharge, effervescing, this the sugar damp where there was pie.

This was before. You slid down the stairs on the belly they would after cut open. He vomited so much I stopped skating. A doctor saw everything, but that was before, and what pulls the mouth of each tube from the gut is a hand. What lowers the diving bell is a system. In the hold some fruit rots. Water held in the mouth will not freeze.

They didn't let us keep anything, we say to each other, our drinks named for a famous surgery and an ongoing siege.

You are kind when you tell me this light is called lily. Not rose, you say, gazing a long time at my description, pressing delete, never rose. I found eyelashes in the dust across the surface of your vanity. The bar was so dark we saw by photograph.

Forsythia had grown over us, a tunnel that ends. When I hold this bloom to your throat, the light matches the photograph.

You pronounce *morning glory* though the bud is sealed. The flower is a site to put light I didn't use in the photograph. At the appearance of the word *document* you shred the flower, an approach to my cunt. You keep a jar of petals, disarticulated and mingling. This plot begins with catastrophe and then memory ends.

When I arrive I know there will be no excavation. The tumor protrudes into the significant air. On the beds no one could sleep, a kettle whistled, toe dragged the luster of cum across the floor.

In this city the faces of roses are swelling.

What I think is sea air is a bay bridges keep finding their way around. The government arrives to each house, not your government, but your house.

In the crowd each figure corresponds to someone from someone's memory. Of this demographic of moment the government keeps no record. Later children will learn how you entered certain dreams. A sort of puddle on the threshold. Journalists will be interested to witness the treads of their shoes cross its face.

On the hill the army stood fairly casually. I swelled with the perception that I was someone's view. The dancing doesn't mean what you think. What kept us awake was not the quickening of history, nor the density of thorns on each stalk.

The new train was as quiet as they'd said, but not for the reasons they'd intimated.

By chance the snow was as blue as the sky I remembered.

Absent of will it wasn't history I'd been believing in, but I gave it up,
I rinsed the jars we'd let blood and pus blend in. Death's twin was
somewhere.

Indeed I knew the scene in which the prince commences his exile,
and for centuries the map is a reverse periplus of ships abandoning
shore.

The map is a wash. One sheet soaked through, it is enough to remem-
ber those before me, the motherhood they held off with an arched
back, keeping pace with the crystalline winters. I'd name each con-
stellation for a coup, but dawn interrupts me.

Is this a coup? we ask each other, our manner learned from shepherds
in poems shepherds never found allegorical. Is this a sheep? and we
follow the trail right into the dripping cave. The historian fell in love
with me suddenly, my vanity suited us, a transference of sentiment in
which he could write of the foothills' slow greening.

The book you would have written was more or less the book you
wrote. It was spring, ice tore back the mud, a scab plucked unripe,
skin at the tongue.

When I reached the end of the map I pronounced it, the word *dis-
placement* an epithet for the fist leaving me, the warmth my hips dis-
covered each time I vanished into the real light of snow.

Another crisis in which all the lawyers marry.

At the behest of security we spat broken bulbs into the album. You unplugged the Christmas tree lights with a gesture meant to remind me you had always been native. You are a native, I said aloud, tasting the phrase once a boy had been kicked off the plane.

There was no carving in the rock face I could call an apology. Beneath blankets the backs of animals.

I lied. I left the stone warming. Beneath blankets a new bloom of pustules. In winter the sea looked gray to the eye.

I knew you amid the long calls of birds hungering, and presently I joined our hands. Later we recalled the syntax that pulled grains of sand into horizon.

No, I never said.

I left it too long.

I was glad to survive and let wind enter through the hospital door. The skin did not break, it just was nearer. I pulled the blanket over me but still you said my name.

Latent

You were walking out of the field,
up some path and to the manor house.
Choose your threshold. Decision is
not a point but a line, a figuring
that incorporates you, enduring
there while dying here, on the stoop
immured, distinct as a book.
Decision is captive. You didn't begin
the field, its acid taste yours again
when a tube gets pulled long from
your own throat. As if sight were
horizonless or you were, a refrain
formed in salt in the still open eyes.
It passes through teeth. If
the field ends it ends in you,
where nothing happens but you,
who are a sweet breach
when the mouth dissolves.

Planned Parenthood

Sidewalk was good

We could all agree on sidewalk

Gather round making shadows

          like a fruit that's

          fruit-sized

I had a good history and wouldn't trade

          it

Insured for or against

In the heat of the

Server farm guessing

          it was like

          NSA had

          a backyard

You understood what was happening as

                                  public noise

                                  like petals bruising themselves

                                  against petals

The essence of fragrance

The difference between coinsurance and

Up every two hours

Someone is calling

                                  it's a sort of tissue

                                  you're distinguishing

                                  through

                                  this way

You said it was statistics but we were

                                  right there

                                  nodding

                                  I feel like I'm nodding

Someone wrote my name slower

capital letters

like I was standing

for something

I think it is a waiting room

Where a TV plays a home renovation show

The host has the same name as you

And is bleeding from the same finger

piss cools

I keep identifying myself as

Waiting

But you said this is when

People will start

good

attempt

A pulse

                              look

                              everyone's ankles

                              are free

Listen, you can see that's a chart

Tell me what it means to you

It's important it means

                                        like that

A sort of technician is saying

Each year the rosebush in the yard blooms

And he gets hired to coach the guy

Through the hearing

Something still red

All these relationships are final

Like dew on the paperwork

Was her hand on your forehead?

Can your father read this?

Is this what it looks like

When I close the door?

Door's closed

Understand

If you can't think one without the other you can't think one

Memory forms at a point,
you said. Where four lines meet,
two lines aren't mine. I said,
memory is a flat plane that casts
a mirror's shadow. You knew the
line of sight, low moon of thumb-
nail to high window, before you
placed me naked behind the glass.
If a face appears in a dream,
I said, it blocks another face.
Morning like a line protruding
into the sky of the present, unlike
the singing of a finger against
the wine glass rim. Your hand
was warm. You cannot govern,
I said, when you feel the archive.
And this disruption suggests
another, triangulating the depths
of something, another jury queued
to enter our conclusive room.
In the mirror was not myself
but a movement along the brink
of what I was. Your cheek was

gone. I said, you forgot what
point it was I called paradise.
You said, you have to learn
to take better care of yourself.

Trophy

I was in the field and this was marked
funereal, an attempt at procession false as
the fear I shouldn't mount a response I don't
want to talk summer days you could see
on the hot asphalt like a map of sisters and mothers
to love a man the police simply killed drones are very
intimate, stories agree of course someone else could have lived
there could have gotten into Yale which is
the University of Arizona of New Haven so many
no-knock warrants and a teacher shot through the hand
there wasn't a sales pitch not really a pregnancy scare but
something simpler like a picture of kids
and who loves them a problem with the luteal phase
there were personal creams for and when I saw her
her dewy tongue and her
status this institutional scent
I recognized what due process

Boarding shortly

A mutual satellite still
locates us   how
at the far sound of wings
you raise an arm
not a metaphor
you objected to but my need
for it   a map
recalling the drift of palimpsest
a line of ambulating tourists
and us   to say nothing
of the war you didn't mean
to stop informing me of
        a taste like soap
over stone before ink effaces
what isn't the text   a site
from what had been your nation
here   as if remembered
lilac as if interrupting
the overnight flight
        I had no instinct
but an artifact of somewhere

you were calling
in photographs   each time
you turned
toward home

Harm reduction

Outrageous as Easter on Twitter, I was saying. Across from me a pigeon stepped across the line of sight of a woman, lying, not asleep, on concrete.

Could she hear me, in my own home, opening a medical bill with one finger? Opening a box of super tampons, green?

The next day I left her a box of super tampons. Green as an ammo box in a row of ammo boxes.

Protein bars, bottles of water. I set them down. The bag whispered. My own phrase is *back to life.*

I say it the day I stop thinking again of suicide. Every liturgical calendar starts pagan and works it out. You can roll back the rock, if you want. You can film it.

A woman can vanish from one place, appear somewhere else. Orange cats pace the sidewalk, indelicate among needles. She lives on the sidewalk, all day I can see her. On the steps of our porches. At night blue lights on our porches keep bodies from finding their own veins.

To fire me someone says to me *this is your last day.*

When you walk by, the bush releases its binders of birds. You go on to have a normal life. You let a family member track your newest patterns on your newest phone.

Why did you change your story? I asked. Like a puff from a muzzle, birds acquit, block after block. Once, when I came, someone asked me *what happened?* Is this how you remember it?

The river was low. It was where the city always dumped us, the crowning dam. There was a small group of volunteers. You could tell they weren't stopping. Most days, I said helpfully, I feel fine.

Did I sound like a cheap canal? Should I stop scrolling?

I want to believe you like a background check believes me, no waiting period. You keep telling me about everything in your file. There's no file. No one thinks there was ever a place like that. I can tell you've been taking selfies of your shadow.

They're converting the old mills to coworking spaces. Things here aren't indelible. Any good party member knows when, by the highway, in the midst of a newspaper, it's coming. Fistful of jacketed birds.

By midday I could get to the library. The key had gone and I knew the return would mean crying out through the chainlink, dialing through the chainlink into a stranger's responsive phone.

I could feel the afternoons in me, fixed as an old case of swayback. At some point I'd get up off the floor and make the wrong dinner. Some mornings a deer stood right before me, looking right at me, and I reached the soft ridge of its spine with the flat of my well-read hand.

People who bother watching you want you to live. When is this true? Are burials cheaper than deportations?

I myself never finished filling out the form. Only the neighborhood knew what to call me. They sent a coyote once down the street and I saw how it went. A dead aunt of my aunt had married so well I could still live. The man was a furrier and all the coats became money well before tastes in bodies changed.

Finally my body began to work for me. I went downtown. In the train station bodies lay right on the steps, unmoving. I went from kiosk to kiosk, pointing. What do you want me to do? a woman said from within the good swells of her uniform. Behind her two more closed their eyes. You must be from the suburbs, she said. What's your plan for the city?

The librarian was shaking his head. This, he said—gesturing toward the book I'd selected—would never shake the UN.

I was starting to remember I'd written the book. Things were coming into focus, like the white etched in an ultrasound becoming a hungering mouth. The library was more like a dairy that's overproduced, valves blasting milk into sewers.

One last time I buttoned my blouse. The ceiling was dreamy and arched, made wholly of glass. After the last war there'd been a rush on transparency. The books had already been catalogued. I'd once believed my own had been spared.

If you were anywhere else, your view, like an egg cracked on the new dome of the city, was just commentary. I knew the feeling, like the dry heat of the professor's hands hovering over the one text I'd read. I thought my neck would smell fresh as a multilith, young and Xeroxed. He had to tell me the war had already begun.

The library was a quiet place to say *the Red Cross was denied access to the camp*. There was a sort of drumbeat and there you go, troops in the protectorate. I felt it all in my ribcage when she was awake. Her face soft as any book. I saw her only when the machine was deployed.

One last time I filled my lungs, like pouring concrete into the ditch of her presence. I would see the librarian at his second job. He knew what he'd do if anything happened to us.

After a few years I found a message you'd left: *I am by the baggage claim. I can't see you.*

What if your invitation was meant for the afterlife?

Our breath was growing short, as if we were walking over the place our forebears had dug the swale. For technical reasons our candidate's name remained on the ballot.

Every car will stop running. Clotheslines are taut above unrepentant violets.

I always knew which day in the cycle.

It's not that I needed the airport to stay open. Or the sheen of tape film between my bluing fingers. I wished there were still a place to not need to speak of you. Only you could hear my voice there, a long storm of hello.

Without a camera I'd have been out of place. I preferred rooftop bars but this was a church basement.

The more you drink, I was saying, the less is left for the troops. Another pour headed my way, sounding just like a soldier pissing on the curve of my boot.

In a generic offering plate I saw my bare torso reflected. I could have dug deeper if asked. The bills heaped up.

When the teardrop hit the nipple, I hit send.

Without the strike we wouldn't have had the strike. I wouldn't have heard you say, *I only speak for myself.*

Your hand was no bigger than mine. Then the white type of end credits, like white phosphorus filling the tunnel. I thought it would be easier. Coming back up the ink was no faster. Say you were not in your accent speaking. No one agrees on the end of the story. No one still here.

Agent

Pencils   shoved in
soil by the grave
erasers in snow

In your book I marked
a passage   rumble of the plow
like the noise of a baby
turning   taste of milk
changes twice   hay
in winter   grass in spring

Flutter names a motion
not a medium   wind or pool
form in blood   some things I knew
just by seeing

Acknowledgments

Gratitude to the editors of the following journals, in which the poems below (often in earlier versions) appeared:

American Poetry Review, "Trophy"
Barnhouse, "Agent" ["Woke late"]
Big Big Wednesday, "Excisions" (full series)
Fairy Tale Review, "Quick flesh"
Fence, "Planned Parenthood," "Canal"
Oversound, "Recall"
Poetry Northwest, "Good news"
Portland Review, "If a gun disappears it reappears," "Startled newspaper," "Accurate sculpture"
Small House Pamphlet Series, no. 1, "Harm reduction" (excerpt)
Sultan's Seal, "Lions"
Territory, "If you can't think one without the other you can't think one"
TYPO, "Ambulances," "Cultivated"
West Branch, "Little autophagy," "Sanctuary on ice"

* * *

This book's epigraph is from *adagio ma non troppo* by Ryoko Sekiguchi, translated by Lindsay Turner, introduction by Sawako Nakayasu (Les Figues Press, 2018). Elsewhere a line appears from Elias Khoury's *Broken Mirrors*, translated by Humphrey Davies (Archipelago Books, 2015).

Warm thanks to Diane Goettel and Black Lawrence Press for offering this book a home and for all their work on behalf of independent literature and publishing.

Thank you to Cleveland and the CSU Poetry Center for asking me (back) into poetry. Thanks to Philadelphia. Michael, MJ, Jacob, Claudia, Mark, Dan, Jess, Tyler, David & Marissa, Roy, Jonathan, Kate, Caren, JP, beautiful friends. Thanks to my mother for her love of poetry. Thank you, Zach.

Photo: Meghan Gallagher

Hilary Plum is the author of several books, including the essay collection *Hole Studies* (Fonograf Editions, 2022), and the novel *Strawberry Fields*, winner of the Fence Modern Prize in Prose (2018). She teaches at Cleveland State University and serves as associate director of the CSU Poetry Center. With Zach Savich she edits the Open Prose Series at Rescue Press.